DATE DUE

MA

Discard

MAR 2 2 2007

TEEN LIFE™

FREQUENTLY ASKED QUESTIONS ABOUT

Identity Theft

Michael R.
Wilson

ROSEN
PUBLISHING®
New York

Published in 2007 by The Rosen Publishing Group, Inc.
29 East 21st Street, New York, NY 10010

Library of Congress Cataloging-in-Publication Data

Wilson, Michael R., 1967–
Frequently asked questions about identity theft/
Michael R. Wilson.—1st ed.
    p. cm.—(FAQ: teen life)
Includes bibliographical references and index.
ISBN-13: 978-1-4042-0964-0
ISBN-10: 1-4042-0964-6 (library binding)
1. Identity theft—United States. 2. Identity theft—United States—
Prevention. I. Title.
HV6679.W55 2007
364.16'3—dc22

                                                    2006018943

Manufactured in the United States of America

Contents

Introduction

You've got to love our high-tech world. Thanks to state-of-the-art computers, high-speed Internet, million-dollar satellites blazing through space, and electronic gadgetry so small and portable, we can bring it with us anywhere we go, staying connected is easier than ever. Cell phones, laptops, and MP3 players are all standard equipment. E-mail, instant messaging, blogs, and chat rooms make communicating a cinch. Online transactions are fast and easy. Phone calls are cheap. Digital technology, as complex as it is, makes life incredibly simple.

But that high-tech world has a drawback. It's dangerous. Predators lurk in chat rooms behind fake names and profiles. Savvy criminals hack into Web sites. Laptop computers and wireless phones, while easily portable, are also easily stolen. There's definitely a downside to digital convenience. You have to stay on your toes. If you don't, you might lose everything.

"Everything" might seem like a lot, maybe even a stretch of the imagination. But picture this: You log on to a Web site, one you've never heard of or seen before, but one that looks cool, certainly worth checking out. You punch in a username and password. You provide some information about yourself—data the site requires for "record-keeping purposes." You type in your address, your phone number, your date of birth. Bingo. You're in.

Today, people can get online just about anywhere—even in a busy cafe. Just don't forget your laptop when you leave!

If you're lucky, that's where it ends. The site is legitimate, and its content is secure. You go on your way, enjoying this new and interesting window on the world. If you're not lucky, however, things have just gotten started. And before you know it, you're in serious trouble. A virus attacks your computer. Your screen goes blank. Your bank account—or that of your parents—is emptied. Or another scenario: Nothing happens, at least not that you can tell. And then one day, perhaps in a month, maybe years down the road, you notice something strange. Someone else is using your name. They've opened accounts in your name, bought a house in your name, and rented cars in your name. You hadn't noticed because you hadn't thought to look. Everything seemed normal.

But now it's clear: You've been duped. Someone, somewhere, has stolen all your personal information and made it his or her own. That person has stolen your identity.

WHAT IS IDENTITY THEFT?

Identity: the distinguishing character or personality of an individual: individuality.

Theft: the act of stealing; specifically the felonious taking and removing of personal property with intent to deprive the rightful owner of it.

—Merriam-Webster's Collegiate Dictionary

Simply put, identity theft is a crime. Just as it's illegal to steal a car or take someone's wallet, it's against the law to steal a person's identity.

Identity theft occurs when one person steals another individual's personal information and then uses that information to do business in the victim's name. The personal information might be a Social Security number, a checking account or driver's license number, a username or password, even an

Credit cards make financial transactions quick and easy, but they're also an easy target for identity thieves looking for personal information.

address or mother's maiden name. Or it might be a combination of some or all of these things. The government, businesses, schools, and employers all use this information for legitimate purposes. They use it to identify people, to determine they are who they say they are, and to maintain accounts that, in theory, only the rightful owner may access. If this information is stolen, the victim's world can be turned upside down.

Identity thieves pretend they are the person whose information they stole. For instance, if an identity thief steals your credit card information, he can then go ahead and use your credit card account, pretending to be you, to purchase things for himself. The bill will go to you.

With your name and Social Security number (SSN), the identity thief can apply for loans, get a driver's license, rent an apartment, purchase utility and telephone services for his new home, or just clean out your financial accounts, telling anyone who asks that he is you. If he gets a traffic ticket, he certainly won't pay it. And why should he? Your name and address are on the books.

When a thief steals your identity, he steals the control you have over your personal financial life. You may lose money, and your credit history—or your chances of getting credit in the first place—may be ruined. But finances aren't all you might lose. You could also temporarily lose your reputation and record as a good citizen. You might ultimately get your life back in order, but not without considerable expense and effort. Identity theft is something to avoid at all costs.

Identity Theft? Or Is It Something Else?

Some experts say that identity theft in the truest sense does not occur nearly as often as people think and that many who believe their identity has been stolen are actually victims of other crimes.

Think about this: If someone steals your checkbook and then goes on to forge several checks in your name, has he stolen your identity? Probably not. More likely, he's borrowed it for a while. By signing your name, he's pretending to be you. But he hasn't done anything to actually take over your personal information, like open new accounts in your name. Most law enforcement agencies would consider that fraud—a serious crime—but not identity theft. The same might be said for someone who steals your credit card or even your ATM card and then goes on a buying spree.

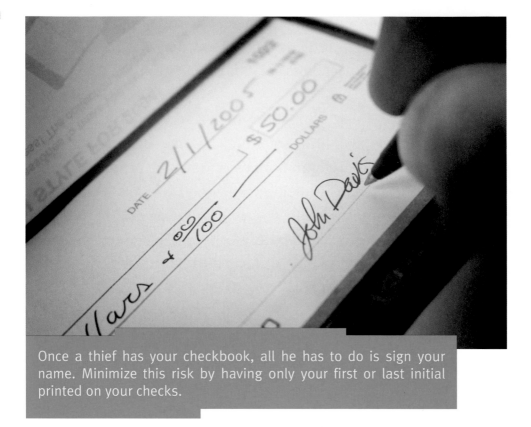

Once a thief has your checkbook, all he has to do is sign your name. Minimize this risk by having only your first or last initial printed on your checks.

Another example is the case of the stolen cell phone. If a thief takes your phone, then makes $300 worth of calls to people you've never met, and you get the bill, you're in for a serious headache. You'll have to resolve the charges with your phone company and convince the company it wasn't you who made the calls. But was your identity stolen? Not really.

So keep this in mind: A lot of crimes are committed today that at first glance look like identity theft but that in reality are nothing more than fraud or plain thievery. It's when someone steals your identifiers—your SSN, your date of birth, your mother's maiden name, and other personal details—and then goes on to establish a new record in your name that your identity has truly been stolen.

What Does a Thief Do with Your Identity?

Once a thief has stolen your identity, there are all kinds of things he can do with it. He can open new credit card accounts in your name and never have to worry about paying his bill. If you happen to already own a credit card, he can make charges on it as well. He might buy expensive items for his own use. Or maybe he'll buy them and then turn around and sell them on the street for cash, which he'll then use to buy drugs.

An identity thief might also use your information to access your savings and checking accounts and to write bad checks in your name. If he's interested, he'll open new bank accounts as well. Maybe he'll transfer money from your legitimate account into his new illegitimate one.

Another thing a thief can do with your information is open new utilities and phone service in your name, for his home. The same goes for cable TV, Internet service, and any other home-based service he might desire.

Sometimes the thief will just need money. If this is the case, perhaps he'll take out a student loan in your name, or a car loan, a business loan, or even a mortgage to pay for a house. Rest assured he'll never pay these loans back. And why should he?

Criminals can use stolen identities for all kinds of things—even big-ticket purchases like a new car.

Some identity thieves will go to the motor vehicle department with the information they've stolen and apply for a new driver's license. A driver's license, with your name and address but their image on the card, can be useful in many different situations. If they are pulled over, you're the one who gets the ticket. If they commit a crime and are arrested, your name goes on the police record. With a driver's license and a few other forms of ID, they can apply for a new passport. And with a passport, they can travel anywhere in the world, all the while passing as you.

Identity Theft on the Rise

Each year, more and more people fall victim to identity theft. According to the Federal Trade Commission (FTC), which keeps track of identity theft occurrence in the United States, in 2005, there were 255,565 registered complaints of identity theft. The FTC tracks other consumer complaints as well. But each year, identity theft tops the list.

The FTC reports that the most common form of identity theft involves credit card fraud (fraud is another word for deception or misrepresentation), where the thief uses stolen information to either buy things with someone else's credit card or establish a new credit card account in the victim's name. Phone or utilities fraud are close seconds, reports the FTC, followed by bank fraud and employment fraud. Most identity theft takes place in the world's major urban areas. And most identity theft victims are under the age of thirty.

Identity theft is on the rise for a number of reasons. The main reason is it's relatively easy to do. With so many people using the Internet for daily transactions and communications, and most of them not thinking twice about the security of those transactions, identity thieves have no shortage of victims they can prey upon.

But the Internet isn't the only place where identity thieves lurk, and it's by no means the most common place for people to have their identity stolen. Other sources of personal information include paper documents that are thrown out in the trash; mail that is intercepted, taken directly from a person's

Myths and Facts
about Identity Theft

Identity theft happens only to careless people.

Fact ➻ Identity theft can happen to anyone, including you. It can even happen if you take the right steps to protect yourself. No one is immune to identity theft.

Identity thieves are always serious, hardened criminals.

Fact ➻ Serious criminals are often the culprits in identity theft cases, but not always. Many identity thieves are friends or even related to their victims. After all, the better someone knows you, the easier it is for him or her to steal your identity.

Victims of identity theft face a lifetime of financial and personal distress. Fact ➻ While no one wants to be an identity theft victim, having your identity stolen is not the end of the world. With a little persistence and a lot of patience, most victims of identity theft can eventually return to their normal lives.

mailbox; and stolen wallets and purses containing credit cards, licenses, insurance information, and other identifying documents. Stolen laptops are full of information useful to the identity thief.

Identity theft incidence is increasing, in other words, because our identities are recorded everywhere. They're on computer, on paper, and on plastic. Identity thieves don't have to look very far to find the information they need.

chapter two

IS MY IDENTITY AT RISK?

Imagine this: You're hanging out at the mall one day with your friends when you come across a booth selling cellular phone service. They're offering a great deal on new phones, but to take advantage of the offer, you must first fill out a form with your name, address, and Social Security number. You complete the form and walk away, expecting your new phone to arrive in the mail. A few weeks later, the phone arrives.

What doesn't arrive—at least not yet—is some bad news: That salesperson, the one in the mall, took your enrollment form and filed it away back at the office. There, a coworker in desperate financial trouble found the form you filled out. He copied your information and then made a few phone calls. Minutes later, he was approved for a new credit card—in your name. Two weeks after, his new card in hand, he charged $3,000 on the account to pay off his

Students and new graduates alike are at risk for identity theft, but it's life after school, as an adult with bills to pay and accounts to manage, where you're most vulnerable.

debts. He has no intention of paying his bill. After all, it is in your name.

If this was real life, your credit rating could be ruined, hurting your chances of obtaining future loans, renting an apartment, or even getting a job. Once you found out about it, it would take months, maybe even years, to clear your name.

Young, but Not Safe

According to the FTC, only 5 percent of identity theft victims are under the age of eighteen. But that number may be misleading.

After all, identity thieves don't care how old you are. They want your identity, not your life experience.

When a teenager—someone like yourself—has her identity stolen, she is far less likely to realize it than an adult. After all, most things that have to do with money are probably taken care of by your parents. You might have a bank account, and maybe you have an ATM card. But you probably don't have a credit card. In fact, it's highly unlikely you have any credit history at all.

When you turn eighteen, though, that will change. At the age of eighteen, most youth are eligible to enter into financial contracts of their own. That means you can legally get a credit card. You can sign a lease to rent an apartment. You can take out a loan to pay for college or buy a car.

For those who have their identity stolen as children, turning eighteen can be a traumatic experience. Just when you think you're ready for the world, you find out that the world already knows you. And its impression of you is not what you think.

Other teens discover their identity has been stolen when they apply for their first driver's license. They go to the motor vehicle department and present their name and SSN, only to find out that someone else has already done the same.

The fact is, there are plenty of ways teens can have their identity stolen. They may not find out about it right away, but they will eventually.

Identity Theft: Easy Money

For the ambitious identity thief, the opportunities for stealing other people's personal information and putting it to use are

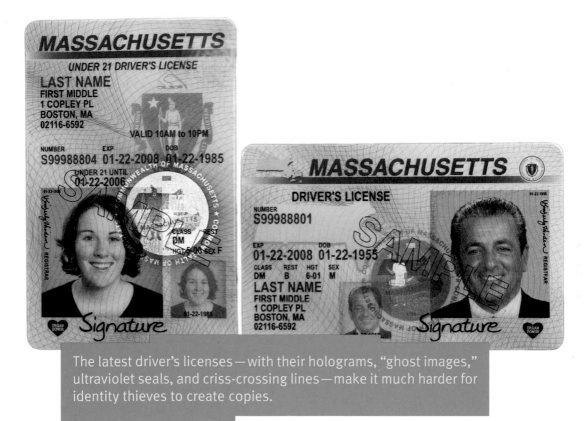

The latest driver's licenses—with their holograms, "ghost images," ultraviolet seals, and criss-crossing lines—make it much harder for identity thieves to create copies.

practically endless. Here are just a few of the ways they go about their (illegal) business. In the next chapter, you'll learn how to protect yourself in each instance.

Dumpster Diving

One common method identity thieves use to steal personal information is as old as identity theft itself: Dumpster diving. Dumpster diving involves literally climbing into Dumpsters—the big metal carts used by garbage trucks—and rummaging through the trash. The thief looks for anything he can use, including

Other people's trash can be a gold mine for potential identity thieves. They look for credit card offers and any other papers that may list personal information.

credit card offers, financial documents, and anything with a name, address, and SSN. A successful dive might yield identifying information for several different people. Dumpster diving has the added advantage of being incredibly simple. You just have to be willing to get dirty. An even easier type of Dumpster diving doesn't even involve the big metal carts. Instead, the ID thief looks through regular trash cans and wastebaskets. In either case, technological know-how is completely unnecessary.

"Friendly Fraud"

So-called "friendly fraud" occurs when a thief steals the identity of a family member, roommate, friend, colleague, or acquaintance. Like Dumpster diving, this means of identity theft is very common, and teens like yourself are particularly susceptible. Sometimes when a mother or father runs into financial trouble and can no

This young man accumulated $50,000 in debt without lifting a finger. How? When he was a teenager, his parents used his Social Security number to open credit card and utility accounts and to take out big loans. Now he's struggling to clear his name.

longer obtain credit in his or her name, he or she will use a son or daughter's information to set up illegal accounts. The child, who relies on his parents for all things money-related, is unlikely to find out—until, that is, he turns eighteen, applies for an account of his own, and is turned down.

Stolen Wallets, Checkbooks, and Credit Cards

A significant portion (around 14 percent, according to the FTC) of identity theft is a result of stolen purses, wallets, bank and credit cards, and checkbooks. Identity thieves use the information they find to set up fraudulent accounts.

Phishing

Phishing (pronounced like the word "fishing") involves the use of e-mail (spam) and illegitimate Web sites and chat rooms to trick Internet users into revealing their personal information—their

10 FACTS ABOUT IDENTITY THEFT

1 An estimated 26 percent of all identity theft involves credit card fraud, or the stealing of a person's credit card information to make unauthorized purchases in that person's name.

2 An estimated 18 percent of all identity theft involves phone or utilities fraud, when the thief establishes phone or utility service in the victim's name.

3 The highest per capita rates of reported identity theft are in the metropolitan areas of Phoenix, Las Vegas, Los Angeles, Dallas, and Miami.

4 Arizona, Nevada, and California are the three states with the highest rates of identity theft.

5 North Dakota is the state with the lowest rate of identity theft.

6 Five percent of all identity theft victims are under age eighteen.

7 An estimated 29 percent of identity theft victims are between the ages of eighteen and twenty-nine.

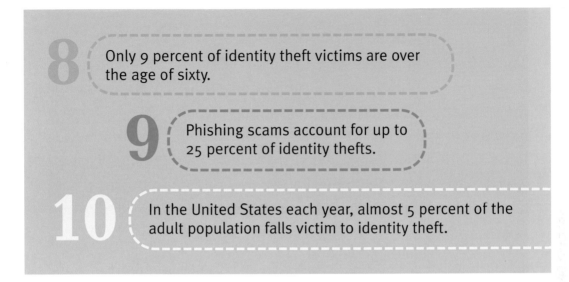

8 Only 9 percent of identity theft victims are over the age of sixty.

9 Phishing scams account for up to 25 percent of identity thefts.

10 In the United States each year, almost 5 percent of the adult population falls victim to identity theft.

address, account numbers, financial information, passwords, and usernames. You might get an e-mail that looks like it comes from your bank or other legitimate financial institution or retailer, when it's actually from a criminal trying to steal your identity.

The e-mail message might express an urgent problem and indicate that immediate action must be taken to correct it. It will ask you to log on and then "validate" or "update" your account information. Meanwhile, everything you type is collected by the identity thief, and before you know it, it's too late.

Online Transactions

Some identity thieves prey on customers of companies that fail to adequately protect their Web sites. If credit card information or other identifying details are not kept under guard, computer-savvy criminals can easily lift whatever they like from such sites.

A Final Word

The answer, then, is yes. You are at risk. Identity theft can happen to anyone, even the most careful among us. It happens to children, it happens to adults, and it happens to the elderly. It even happens to the dead, who leave all kinds of unprotected identifying information behind when they pass. There is no foolproof way to keep your identity protected and eliminate this risk. The best you can do is to minimize your chances of becoming the next victim.

three

HOW CAN I PROTECT MY IDENTITY?

Some experts believe teens are more vulnerable to identity theft than most of the adult population because they spend more time online. Teens, they say, tend not to think as much about their personal safety and vulnerability when surfing the Internet. Teens are also more vulnerable, the theory goes, because they're far less likely to check their credit reports. Prove the "experts" wrong. Stay on top of things and guard your identity like a pro.

That said, most of the measures that protect your identity are out of your control. Legitimate companies, for instance, use encryption technology to ensure that transactions conducted on their Web sites are safe and secure from thieves. Encryption technology scrambles and codes the information you submit to the site, preventing prying eyes from seeing what they should not.

Facial recognition is a type of biometric technology used to ensure people are who they claim to be.

Companies are also required to follow certain rules and regulations designed to protect consumers from identity theft. When a customer calls his credit card company, for instance, he's required to provide the company with certain details of his account that only he would know before he is allowed access to that account.

The problem, of course, is when those details are already known by the identity thief. And that's where you can take steps to keep your identity safe. Here are some tips.

When Online . . .

News reports would make you think that the Internet is a dangerous place to do business. And it is—if you're not careful.

Anyone with a computer and a connection to the Internet can create a Web site and call it a business. For the most part, these Internet operations are legitimate and fair. But the world is full of crooks—and the Internet is an easy tool for them to get rich quick.

Use Protective Software

The most important thing you can do to protect yourself and your computer when you go online is to use anti-virus software and a firewall and keep all protective software up to date. Such software will prevent criminals from hacking into your computer, installing secret programs that record your keystrokes, and stealing personal information straight from your desktop. You should also install all security patches provided by the maker of your computer operating system.

Do Business on Secure Web Sites

When you do submit personal information on a Web site, make sure the site is secure. You'll see "https" in the URL. This means the Web site employs Secure Socket Layer (SSL) technology to protect users. You might also see a lock icon in the lower corner of your screen.

If you have any doubt whether a Web site is secure, or fear the site may be a scam, contact the Better Business Bureau (BBB). The BBB maintains a list of companies that have been reported as fraudulent and can let you know whether it's safe to conduct transactions with a particular business.

Legitimate Web sites will provide you with information on their privacy policy about how they protect users. Most reputable sites will also list business contact information such as an address and phone number. Read everything. If it doesn't seem safe, go elsewhere.

Watch Out for Phishing

When it comes to Internet-based identity theft, phishing is by far the most common way for thieves to attract new victims. Some experts believe phishing accounts for up to 25 percent of all identity theft cases.

How can you avoid falling prey to phishers? Never open an e-mail attachment if the sender is unfamiliar to you. Some attachments contain programs that are automatically (and secretly) downloaded onto your computer. Once installed, they record your keystrokes as you type. This is one way phishers can steal your passwords or other sensitive information.

A legitimate financial institution will never request that you send sensitive information in an e-mail. If you believe an e-mail is from a phisher, delete it immediately. If the e-mail appears to be from a legitimate institution, but you're not 100 percent sure, contact that institution by phone to confirm before replying to it. Don't use any phone numbers provided in the e-mail. Instead, check a billing statement for the number or use a phone book. You can also log on to the correct Web site by typing the legitimate site address directly into your browser window. The bottom line: When in doubt, don't do it.

A few years ago, Mark Nicols, of Crosby, North Dakota, fell prey to an e-mail scam. The scam tricked him into revealing his eBay password and other personal information on a fake Web site run by identity thieves.

Chat Room Etiquette

The rule for chat rooms is simple: Never give a fellow chat room user your personal information. You can never be sure who you're dealing with.

Use Good Passwords

Spend any time online, and before you know it, you'll have dozens of passwords and usernames to remember. Passwords prevent other people from accessing your account. For this reason, it's important to choose good passwords and to change them regularly.

How can you create a good password? One idea is to think of a memorable phrase, take the first letter from each word, and then convert some of the letters in the phrase to numbers that look like letters or to numbers that correspond to the letter's position in the alphabet. For example, "I like pizza" could become 1L1kePi26z1 (the first two *I*'s become 1's because they look the same; the first *z* becomes 26, which is that letter's position in the alphabet; the *a* becomes 1 because it's the first letter in the alphabet). Mix capital and lowercase letters, symbols (@, #, $), and numbers. Never use your mother's maiden name in a password or in any other capacity. With that information, a criminal can go on to obtain a birth certificate in your name, and from there to get a Social Security card, passport, driver's license, and other documents. Never use a phone number, address, SSN, or even part of your SSN in your password. And be sure to use different passwords for different accounts.

Remembering your passwords may prove difficult, especially when they start to add up. Keep a list of your passwords in a safe place (not your wallet), and look them up if you forget them.

Guard Your Possessions

Identity thieves prey on careless people. When out and about, watch your stuff. Cell phones, driver's licenses, checkbooks, passports, credit cards, bank cards—you get the picture. If it's potentially valuable, thieves will try to steal it.

If you carry a wallet or purse, keep in it only what you absolutely need for the day (your school ID, for instance). Don't carry extra cards that could possibly be used by an identity thief.

Laptops, cell phones, pagers, and MP3 players are all targeted by identity thieves for the personal information that may be stored on them. Always use key-lock features and a strong password to protect these devices, and keep a close eye on everything to prevent them from being stolen in the first place. Laptops are particularly tempting to identity thieves. Because laptops are portable, they're also easy to steal. Always log off your laptop when you're done using it, and never use automatic log-in features that save your username and password. Most of all, keep your laptop under close guard whenever you use it in public.

Desktop computers, while less likely to be stolen, also require precautions. Again, use passwords to guard your information.

Before you sell or give a used computer to another person, or dispose of an old, outdated computer, first delete all personal information contained on it. This is not as easy as it sounds. Dragging files to the trash is unlikely to do the job. Instead, use a "wipe" utility program to overwrite the hard drive.

At home, be sure your doors and windows are locked when nobody's around. If your house has an alarm system, use it. Personal information kept at home should be locked away where it's hard to access—in a filing cabinet or safe.

Paperwork

Identity thieves will often look for discarded financial documents, receipts, credit card applications, insurance forms, and

Paper-shredding is one way to make sure identity thieves can't read your discarded personal documents. A pile of shredded paper would take years—if not forever—to reassemble into something readable.

other papers that include personal information they can use. Prevent prying eyes from getting to your documents by using a paper shredder. You can buy a shredder at a home office supply store. The best shredders are of the "cross-cut" variety. These shred papers into tiny pieces instead of strips (which in theory could be patched back together, but in truth do a perfectly adequate job for most purposes).

Unprotected mailboxes are an identity thief's best friend. It's very easy for a thief to walk up to your box, open it up, and pull

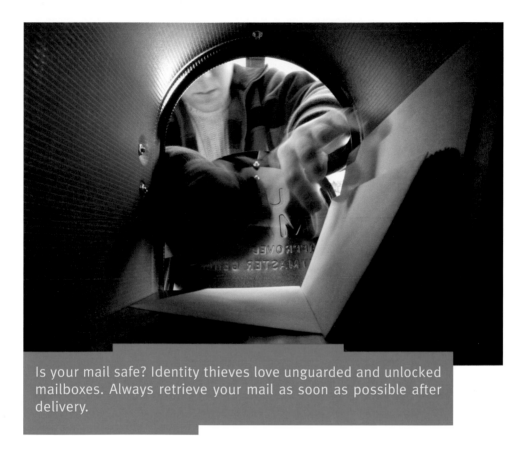

Is your mail safe? Identity thieves love unguarded and unlocked mailboxes. Always retrieve your mail as soon as possible after delivery.

out your mail. Once he has your mail, there's no telling what he might find—credit card offers, bank statements, utility or phone bills with your data all over them, or any number of other potentially important documents.

What can you do to protect your mail? First, never use an unsecured mailbox to send important outgoing mail. Instead, use an official post office collection box with a one-way mail slot, or mail such items directly through the post office. Second, if you receive your mail in an open (non-lockable) mailbox, retrieve it each day as soon as possible following delivery. If you'll be away for some time—as you might during a family vacation—ask a friend or neighbor to pick up your mail for you and hold it until you return, or call the U.S. Postal Service (800-275-8777) and ask it to do the same. The idea is to avoid leaving your mail in an unprotected spot long enough for a thief to steal it.

You should also beware of the things you receive in the mail. Identity thieves will sometimes target unsuspecting people through fake promotional offers mailed to their homes. If something arrives in the mail that looks suspicious or too good to be true, in most cases it's best to just shred it.

Last but not least, review all financial statements, like those from your bank, whenever you receive them. If you see any problems or irregularities, report them to the institution with which you have your account.

Watch Your Words

A good rule of thumb: Never offer personal information to a telephone solicitor. You should only give credit card information or other personal details if you initiate the call. It may seem like that telemarketer has good intentions, but he could be trying to take you for a ride.

Solicitors may also approach the front door of your home. Again, salespeople or other solicitors may be legitimate, but unless you personally know the company or organization they claim to represent, you have every right to be suspicious.

Guard Your Numbers

We live in a world full of numbers. Many of those numbers are used for identification purposes. It's important, therefore, to guard yours. Keep them to yourself, and reveal them only when you absolutely have to.

Your most important number, by far, is your SSN. SSNs are assigned to citizens, permanent residents, and some temporary residents by the Social Security Administration, a branch of the U.S. government. The number is used for tax purposes and to keep track of an individual's Social Security benefits.

Because everyone has their own SSN, many companies, agencies, and organizations like to use it as an identification number. In the hands of an identity thief, however, an SSN is a free ticket to a new life.

How can you protect your SSN? You can begin with your Social Security card. If you have a card, don't carry it around with you. You'll need it only rarely in your life, so keep it in a secure place at home. Lock it up in a safe along with your birth certificate, or keep it in a safe-deposit box at your bank.

After the card itself is safe, it's up to you to protect your number. Reveal it only when you absolutely have to. If a business or organization asks for it, ask the organization why it needs it, how it plans to protect it from others, and whether it would be possible to substitute another means of identification instead. When it comes to school IDs, insist that they not print your SSN on your card.

Likewise, when you apply for your driver's license, make sure your SSN won't be printed on the card. Most states don't use SSNs anymore, but if you're in a state that does, see if you can use a different number instead.

The same can be said for any form of identification that you could potentially lose or have stolen. Checks, for example, should not include your SSN with your name and address.

When you apply for your first job, your prospective employer may ask you for your SSN. You don't have to provide it at this point, and you shouldn't. Say you don't know it or that you'd prefer not to provide it, and that you'll give it once you're hired.

If you are hired, you will need to provide your SSN for wage and tax reporting purposes. Your employer will use your SSN to inform the IRS how much money you made and what taxes were withheld from your paychecks. Later, when it comes time for your tax refund, the IRS will use your number to determine how much money to send to you.

As you get older, there will be times when you'll need to supply your SSN to companies who want to know about your credit history before they will give you a loan, hook up your utilities, rent an apartment to you, or conduct other business with you. In these cases, you have no choice but to supply your number.

WHAT SHOULD I DO IF MY IDENTITY IS STOLEN?

Are you a victim of identity theft? If the answer is yes, don't panic. Just do what you have to do to minimize the damage.

How to Tell If You're a Victim

First things first. You can't respond to identity theft unless you're aware your identity has been stolen. A few potential giveaways:

If you start receiving credit offers in the mail but you have no credit history that you're aware of, your identity may have been stolen. Unsolicited credit card offers are given only to those with credit histories. Likewise, if you receive bank statements or other financial correspondence from an institution you've never heard of, be suspicious.

If you apply for your driver's license and you discover that another license has already been issued in your

Most of the direct mail being sorted at this warehouse for distribution comes from legitimate businesses. Sometimes, however, identity thieves will use professional-looking marketing materials to trick unsuspecting readers into revealing personal information.

name, but to somebody else, your identity may have been stolen. There is a slim chance there is someone else with your name or there was some sort of mix-up, but it's unlikely.

If you apply for a student loan, a credit card (if you're eighteen years old), or to any other lender and you are denied despite the fact that you believe you are qualified, you may have an identity theft problem.

If telemarketers start calling you, it may be that someone stole your identity and now telemarketers are trying to sell

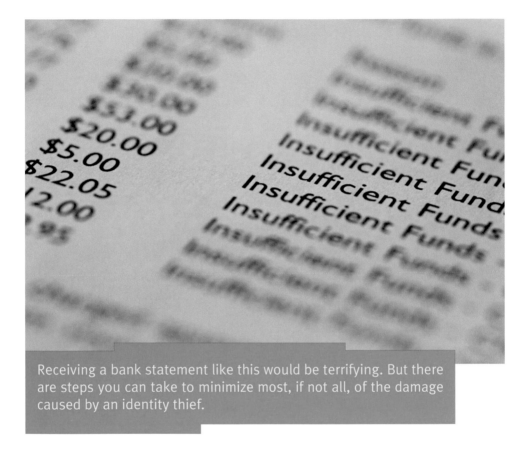

Receiving a bank statement like this would be terrifying. But there are steps you can take to minimize most, if not all, of the damage caused by an identity thief.

you things because they believe *you're* the one with the history of credit.

If you don't receive mail that you're accustomed to receiving, you may be a victim of identity theft. If bank statements, for instance, stop arriving at your house, or credit card statements (if you have a credit card) never show up, someone may have taken over your accounts.

If people identifying themselves as debt collectors call your house or knock on your door, you may have identity theft issues.

Ten Great Questions to Ask If You Think Your Identity Has Been Stolen

1 Am I in any immediate danger, and if so, how can I get to safety?

2 Are there any clues as to how my identity was stolen or who the perpetrator is?

3 What financial accounts do I have open, and how can I contact the institutions that manage those accounts to let them know I am a victim of identity theft?

4 What government-issued documents—Social Security number, driver's license, etc.—may have been compromised, and how can I contact the appropriate agencies to cancel them and receive replacements?

5 How can I file reports on the theft with my local police department and the Federal Trade Commission?

6 How can I get a copy of my credit report, which may provide more details on the extent of the theft?

7 Are there any signs of identity theft on my credit report—including fraudulent or inaccurate information—and if so, what should I do?

8 How can I close any accounts that were tampered with or opened fraudulently in my name?

9 How can I reestablish my identity as quickly as possible?

10 How can I prevent identity theft from happening again?

Credit Reports

The best way to tell if you're a victim of identity theft is by monitoring your credit reports. Thanks to the Fair Credit Reporting Act (FCRA), everyone is eligible to receive one free credit report from each of the three major credit reporting companies every year. Take advantage of this. Ask for yours.

Of course, if you don't own a credit card or have never taken a bank loan, when you ask for a credit report you should be told that none exists. On the other hand, if you receive a report despite a lack of credit history, someone may have established credit in your name.

The three credit reporting companies are Equifax, Experian, and TransUnion. There are other companies as well, and you'll see them advertised online, but you shouldn't deal with them. In some cases, they might even be fake reporting companies existing solely to steal your identity.

You can order a free report from any or all of the three major companies. Most identity theft experts recommend ordering one

President George W. Bush signs federal legislation that gives consumers protections against identity theft on December 4, 2003. Free credit reports and a national fraud-alert system are among the latest developments.

from each, just in case one company picked something up that the other two missed. To do so, go to http://www.annualcreditreport. com, or call (877) 322-8228. Requesting a report by phone takes about five minutes. You can also go to http://www.ftc.gov/credit to obtain an Annual Credit Report Request Form, which you can print, fill out, and mail to Annual Credit Report Request Service, P.O. Box 105281, Atlanta, GA 30348-5281. The companies will not provide free reports to people who call them directly.

Your credit report will include information on where you live, your bill payment history if you have one (do you pay on time?),

It's rarely any fun to pay bills. But keeping close tabs on your personal finances is a good way to prevent identity theft.

and information on whether you've ever been in financial trouble. Credit information is sold by the reporting companies to creditors, employers, and businesses so they can evaluate you and decide whether to do business with you. These are all things you'll have to worry about once you're responsible for your own finances—and when you apply for credit, insurance, or to rent or buy a house or car, for example. Until then, your report should be thin, if it exists at all.

Examine your credit report closely, making sure all the details are accurate. If you find any mistakes, contact the reporting company immediately.

Take Action

The Federal Trade Commission recommends you take the following actions as soon as you realize you're a victim of identity theft:

1. Put a fraud alert on your credit reports, then review those reports

First, place a fraud alert on your credit reports. Any of the three consumer reporting companies can provide you with information on how to place a fraud alert. You only need to place one alert. The company with which you place the alert will inform the other two of the situation.

Here's the fraud alert contact information for each company:

Equifax
P.O. Box 740241
Atlanta, GA 30374-0241
(800) 525-6285
www.equifax.com

Experian
P.O. Box 9532
Allen, TX 75013
(888) 397-3742
www.experian.com

TransUnion
Fraud Victim Assistance Division
P.O. Box 6790
Fullerton, CA 92834-6790
(800) 680-7289
www.transunion.com

Next, order free copies of your credit reports from the three reporting companies. Maybe you realized you were a victim of identity theft when you looked at those reports earlier. If you learned some other way, now is the time to check your reports for further evidence of theft. When you get the reports, look them over very closely. Make sure that all information is correct and that all accounts listed are in fact your own. If you find anything that looks suspicious or is outright wrong, look into it and, if necessary, have it corrected and removed from your report. Request all corrections in writing by contacting the credit reporting companies directly.

2. Close accounts that have been accessed by the thief or opened in your name

Accounts that may have been compromised include those for credit cards, banking, utilities, cell phones, and Internet service, among others. Close any accounts that have been accessed by the identity thief or fraudulently opened in your name. The contact information for companies maintaining accounts in your name will be listed on your credit report. Call each company and ask for the security or fraud department. Keep track of your conversations and correspondence. Always follow up in writing. For example, if you need to close a bank account, first call the bank and ask them to close the account. Then send a letter by certified mail informing them of your request. Make copies of all paperwork, and keep all correspondence on file.

As you close down your old accounts, you can open new ones. Just be sure to use new passwords and PINs. For tips on how to choose safe passwords, see the previous chapter.

3. If your checking or bank accounts have been accessed, report it to the bank

Contact your bank immediately, as it's only a matter of time before the thief taps into your savings and checking accounts. Talk to the bank manager to determine what steps to take to protect or to safely reestablish your accounts.

4. Report the theft to the police

To start the hunt for the thief, file a report at your local police station. It's unlikely they'll find the perpetrator, but you never know.

5. Contact the FTC

The Federal Trade Commission tracks identity thefts and does what it can to convict identity thieves of their crimes. Call the FTC Identity Theft Hotline toll-free at (877) ID-THEFT (438-4388); TDD (866) 653-4261.

You can also reach the FTC through its Web site, http://www.ftc.gov, or by mail. Write to:

Identity Theft Clearinghouse
Federal Trade Commission
600 Pennsylvania Avenue NW
Washington, DC 20580

HOW CAN I REESTABLISH MY IDENTITY?

You've stopped the ship from sinking; now it's time to repair all the damage. The steps you took from the previous chapter are a great start, and they should prevent the identity thief from continuing to use your private information for personal gain. But don't believe for a moment that you're entirely in the clear. It will take considerable time and effort to put your world back in order.

First Step: Keeping Tabs

From now on, you'll need to monitor absolutely every detail of your credit report. Check your credit reports once every three months for the first year following the theft, and then once per year after that.

Also be sure to read all financial statements (bank statements, for example) as soon as you receive them.

In 2005, Brandon Monchamp, of Scottsdale, Arizona, pleaded guilty to running a Web site that offered stolen credit cards, bank cards, and personal identity information to anyone who wanted it. The Internet has made it easy for criminals to practice their illegal trade. They usually—but not always—get away with it.

If anything looks suspicious, report it immediately.

Beware of other signs of identity theft recurrence as well (see previous chapter). You can never be too vigilant, especially if you've already fallen victim to identity theft. You don't want it to happen again.

Money Issues

If you lost money due to identity theft, certain state and federal laws may apply that will limit your liability and help you get your money back.

Which laws apply depends on the specific crimes that were committed. The Electronic Funds Transfer Act, for example, is a federal law that protects consumers who lost money through fraudulent use of an ATM or debit card. You may be liable for $50 or $100 of the total amount of money that was stolen. Or you may not be liable for any of it.

To ensure you get as much money back as possible, it's important to report signs of fraud to financial institutions right away, in writing, and to keep written records of all interactions with customer representatives (name, date, basic details about your conversation). Keep copies of letters that you send, and file paper records away in a safe place. You never know when you may need them again. Financial institutions should be able to walk you through the specific steps you must take to get your money back.

Clearing Your Name

Some identity theft victims find that crimes have been committed in their names. If, when you contact your police department, you discover there's a warrant out for your arrest, you'll need to take steps to clear your name.

You can do so by going to the police department and filing an impersonation report to confirm your identity and wipe your record clean. You may also need to contact the court that issued the warrant for the person's arrest. Get details at the police station.

You should also contact your state motor vehicle department if you suspect a thief has used your information to get a driver's license in your name. Your motor vehicle department can walk you through the steps required to correct any problems.

If your SSN was stolen and used in the identity theft and you're under eighteen (and therefore don't have a credit history of your own), it may be worth applying for a new number.

One identity theft ring in Southern California is believed to have stolen millions of dollars from unsuspecting people. Police surveillance and raids brought the ring to justice.

You can do so by contacting the Social Security Administration. Go to www.socialsecurity.gov, or call (800) 772-1213 for more information.

Ultimately, you may need the help of adults that you know and trust, and you may even need a lawyer to help you through the legal details of reestablishing your identity. Be patient, don't give up, and realize it's not your fault. In the end it will all work out.

CARRIE'S STORY

Carrie never saw it coming. A senior in high school, just seventeen years old, she'd finally taken the SAT and was waiting to hear from colleges. Her grades were good, and her references were perfect. She had everything going for her.

That's when everything fell apart. The acceptance letters came, but with them came a caveat: no financial aid. Carrie's family had no money. She couldn't afford to pay for school herself. There was no reason for schools not to offer her loans. Or was there?

Carrie looked into it. Her loan applications were rejected, she was told, for her poor credit history. Her history, the colleges said, showed she never paid her bills. She owed at least five different companies thousands of dollars. Check your credit report, they told her. The proof's right there.

This took Carrie by surprise. She'd never had credit before. She'd never even had bills of her own. She'd never used anything but cash—the money she earned as a lifeguard each summer. How could she have a credit history? What was going on?

A little more investigating, and Carrie had her answer. Her credit report, which, on advice from a teacher, she ordered through the Federal Trade Commission, made it clear: Someone had stolen her identity. They'd posed as her to get credit cards in her name, open utility accounts, and even take out a loan to buy a car. Someone, somewhere, was pretending to be her. And now Carrie was paying for it.

(Continued on next page)

(Continued from previous page)

Carrie was no pushover. She'd made it through high school and was headed for college, thanks to hard work and perseverance. She wasn't about to let a stranger ruin everything.

Following the FTC's advice, she took action. She put a fraud alert on her credit report. She reported the theft to authorities, including the police. She closed the fraudulent accounts. And then, because she knew college depended on it, she called her top pick's financial aid office.

It took some explaining, but before long, Carrie was in the clear. Her application for financial aid was reviewed. And within a month, she'd received the letter she was looking for: She'd been approved, and the money was on its way. She was going to college.

Weeks later, the ordeal all but behind her, Carrie received a phone call. It was the police. Her identity, they said, had been stolen by a person she worked with during the summer. The man had lifted her Social Security number and other personal details from a filing cabinet that contained her work application. He'd done the same to at least three other employees. And now he was going to jail.

Don't Let It Happen Again

Most important, do everything you can to avoid falling prey to identity theft all over again. Change all of your passwords and PINs, and continue to change them on a regular basis. Keep your eyes peeled for suspicious activity related to your accounts. Monitor everything.

Victims of identity theft often have trouble proving they are who they say they are. "Identity theft passports" like this one are sometimes issued by local authorities to help such people make the transition back to a normal life.

For more information, including all the details you'll ever need to reestablish your identity and prevent it from happening again, go to the Federal Trade Commission Web site at http://www.ftc.gov. For more identity theft resources, see the For More Information section at the end of this book.

Glossary

chat room A place online where users can "talk" and easily communicate with other people in real time.

credit history Personal record of credit use, including whether financial loans have been paid back according to agreements.

credit report Document that includes a thorough record of an individual's financial and credit histories.

Dumpster diving Technique used by individuals to retrieve anything from food to personal documents from an open trash receptacle.

Federal Trade Commission (FTC) Government agency responsible for protecting consumers from fraudulent and illegal business practices.

financial Having to do with money.

fraud Trickery or deception.

fraud alert An official notice submitted to credit reporting companies that one's private, personal information has been stolen or otherwise compromised.

fraudulent Characterized by fraud or deception.

friendly fraud Fraud committed against an individual who the perpetrator knows.

identity Individuality.

password Series of letters, numbers, and/or symbols required for access to personal information, accounts, or property.

personal Private.

personal identification number (PIN) Special number required for access to personal accounts.

phishing Use of e-mails and illegitimate Web sites to trick Internet users into revealing their personal information.

Secure Socket Layer (SSL) Technology used by legitimate Web sites to protect users from fraud.

shredder Electronic device that shreds unwanted paper documents into tiny, unreadable strips or pieces.

Social Security number (SSN) Number assigned to citizens, permanent residents, and some temporary residents by the Social Security Administration, a branch of the U.S. government. The number is used for tax purposes and to keep track of an individual's Social Security benefits. It is also used for identification purposes.

spam Unwanted, mass-delivered e-mail.

Federal Bureau of Investigation
J. Edgar Hoover Building
935 Pennsylvania Avenue NW
Washington, DC 20535-0001
(202) 324-3000
Web site: http://www.fbi.gov
  The FBI is the law enforcement agency of the U.S. government that investigates violations and criminal acts
  against the United States, including identity theft.

Federal Trade Commission
600 Pennsylvania Avenue NW
Washington, DC 20580
(202) 382-4357
Web site: http://www.consumer.gov/idtheft
  The FTC is a government agency that works to protect
  consumers from fraudulent, deceptive, and unfair business practices.

Identity Theft Resource Center
P.O. Box 26833
San Diego, CA 92196
(858) 693-7935
E-mail: itrc@idtheftcenter.org
Web site: http://www.idtheftcenter.org

ITRC is a nonprofit program providing support to consumers and victims of identity theft, as well as advice on the subject to governmental agencies, legislators, and companies.

Privacy Rights Clearing House
3100 5th Avenue, Suite B
San Diego, CA 92103
(619) 298-3396
Web site: http://www.privacyrights.org
This nonprofit consumer advocacy organization works to raise consumer awareness of how technology affects personal privacy. It also finds ways to empower consumers to control their personal information by suggesting practical ways to protect privacy.

U.S. Department of Justice
950 Pennsylvania Avenue NW
Washington, DC 20530-0001
(202) 514-2000
E-mail: askdoj@usdoj.gov
Web site: http://www.usdoj.gov/criminal/fraud/idtheft.html
The Department of Justice is the law enforcement arm of the U.S. government.

Hotlines
FTC Identity Theft Hotline
(877) ID-THEFT

Social Security Administration Fraud Hotline
(800) 269-0271

Credit Report Companies

Equifax Fraud Division
P.O. Box 740250
Atlanta, GA 30374
(800) 525-6285

Experian Fraud Division
P.O. Box 1017
Allen, TX 75013
(888) 397-3742

TransUnion Fraud Division
P.O. Box 6790
Fullerton, CA 92634
(800) 680-7289

Web Site

Due to the changing nature of Internet links, Rosen Publishing has developed an online list of Web sites related to the subject of this book. This site is updated regularly. Please use this link to access the list

http://www.rosenlinks.com/faq/idth

For Further Reading

Arata, Michael. *Preventing Identity Theft for Dummies.*
    Indianapolis, IN: Wiley Publishing, Inc., 2004.
Hammond, Robert. *Identity Theft: How to Protect Your Most
    Valuable Asset.* Franklin Lakes, NJ: Career Press, 2003.
Silver Lake Publishing Editors. *Identity Theft.* Aberdeen,
    WA: Silver Lake Publishing, 2004.
Sullivan, Bob. *Your Evil Twin: Behind the Identity Theft
    Epidemic.* Hoboken, NJ: John Wiley & Sons, 2004.
Welsh, Amanda. *The Identity Theft Protection Guide.* New
    York, NY: St. Martin's Press, 2004.

Bibliography

Federal Trade Commission. "Consumer Fraud and Identity Theft Complaint Data, January–December 2005." January 2006. Retrieved February 13, 2006 (http://www.consumer.gov/sentinel/pubs/Top10Fraud2005.pdf).

Federal Trade Commission. "ID Theft." Retrieved February 18, 2006 (http://www.consumer.gov/idtheft).

Federal Trade Commission. "Remedying the Effects of Identity Theft." Retrieved February 13, 2006 (http://www.ftc.gov/bcp/conline/pubs/credit/idtsummary.pdf).

Federal Trade Commission. "Take Charge: Fighting Back Against Identity Theft." February 2005. Retrieved February 18, 2006 (http://www.ftc.gov/bcp/conline/pubs/credit/idtheft.htm).

Federal Trade Commission. "What to Do If Your Personal Information Has Been Compromised." March 2005. Retrieved March 28, 2006 (http://www.ftc.gov/bcp/conline/pubs/alerts/infocompalrt.htm).

Fight Identity Theft. "Are You a Victim of Identity Theft?" 2001–2006. Retrieved March 29, 2006 (http://www.fightidentitytheft.com/identity_theft_learn.html).

Fight Identity Theft. "Think You're Already a Victim? Follow These Seven Steps." 2001–2006. Retrieved March 29, 2006 (http://www.fightidentitytheft.com/identity_theft_victim.html).

Identity Theft Resource Center. "Identity Theft and Children."
    August 2003. Retrieved April 14, 2006 (http://www.
    idtheftcenter.org/vg120.html).
Privacy Rights Clearing House. 1996–2005. Retrieved March 30,
    2006 (http://www.privacyrights.org/identity.htm).
Qwest Communications. "Don't Get Ripped Off! Identity Theft
    Tips for Teens." 2004. Retrieved April 9, 2006 (http://
    www.qwest.com/highwayqwest/identitytheft/index.html).
Qwest Communications. "Quest's Consumer Protection
    Resource Guide." 2006. Retrieved April 12, 2006 (http://
    www.qwest.com/about/protection/index.html).

Index

About the Author

Michael R. Wilson is a writer, editor, and photographer. He has written numerous books as well as articles for both print publications and online.

Photo Credits

Cover © www.istockphoto.com/Amanda Rohde; p. 5 © Justin Sullivan/Getty Images; p. 8 © www.istockphoto.com/Silvia Bukovac; p. 10 © www.istockphoto.com/Sean Locke; p. 12 © Franco Vogt/Corbis; p. 17 Stephen Coburn/Shutterstock.com; p. 19 © Elise Amendola/AP/Wide World Photos; p. 20 © Larry Powell/Shutterstock; p. 21 © Jerry S. Mendoza/AP/Wide World Photos; p. 26 © Ian Waldie/Getty Images; p. 29 © Don Anderson/AP/Wide World Photos; p. 32 © Tom Olmscheid/AP/Wide World Photos; p. 33 Greg McCracken/Shutterstock.com; p. 38 © Steve Miller/AP/Wide World Photos; p. 39 © Philip James Corwin/Corbis; p. 42 © Ron Edmonds/AP/Wide World Photos; p. 43 © Francisco Cruz/SuperStock; p. 48 © Mike Derer/AP/Wide World Photos; p. 50 © Reed Saxon/AP/Wide World Photos; p. 53 © Rogelio Solis/AP/Wide World Photos.

Editor: Leigh Ann Cobb; Series Designer: Evelyn Horovicz
Photo Researcher: Hillary Arnold